M782.24 Bach.J Six

Bach, Johann Sebastian, 1685-1750.
Six great secular cantatas : in full score.

DATE DUE

| | |
|---|---|
| DEC 1 9 2001 | |
| JAN 2 4 2007 | |
| | |
| JUL 0 2 2007 | |
| 7/30/2007 | |
| NOV 2 0 2007 | |
| | |
| | |
| | |
| | |

DEMCO, INC. 38-2931

# Johann Sebastian Bach
# SIX GREAT SECULAR CANTATAS

In Full Score

From the
Bach-Gesellschaft
Edition

DOVER PUBLICATIONS, INC.
NEW YORK

# CONTENTS

| CANTATA | Page |
|---|---|
| "WAS MIR BEHAGT, IST NUR DIE MUNTRE JAGD"; 1716 (Hunt Cantata; No. 208; for the birthday of Duke Christian of Sachsen-Weissenfels; text by Salomo Franck) | 1 |
| "WEICHET NUR, BETRÜBTE SCHATTEN"; ca. 1720 (Wedding Cantata; No. 202; soprano solo) | 41 |
| "ZERREISSET, ZERSPRENGET, ZERTRÜMMERT DIE GRUFT"; 1725 (Der zufriedengestellte Aeolus [Aeolus Appeased]; No. 205; for the name-day of August Friedrich Müller, doctor of philosophy at the University of Leipzig; text by Picander [Christian Friedrich Henrici]) | 57 |
| "GESCHWINDE, IHR WIRBELNDEN WINDE"; ca. 1731 (Der Streit zwischen Phoebus und Pan [The Quarrel Between Phoebus and Pan]; No. 201; text by Picander) | 147 |
| "SCHWEIGT STILLE, PLAUDERT NICHT"; ca. 1732 (Coffee Cantata; No. 211; for soprano, tenor and bass; text by Picander) | 217 |
| "MER HAHN EN NEUE OBERKEET"; 1742 (Peasant Cantata; No. 212; for soprano and bass; in honor of Saxon chamberlain Carl Heinrich von Dieskau as new lord of the manor Klein-Zschocher; text by Picander) | 249 |
| TRANSLATION OF TEXTS | 281 |

---

Copyright © 1980 by Dover Publications, Inc.
All rights reserved under Pan American and International Copyright Conventions.

Published in Canada by General Publishing Company, Ltd., 30 Lesmill Road, Don Mills, Toronto, Ontario.
Published in the United Kingdom by Constable and Company, Ltd., 10 Orange Street, London WC2H 7EG.

This Dover edition, first published in 1980, is an unabridged republication of six cantatas from two volumes of *Johann Sebastian Bach's Werke*, originally published by the Bach-Gesellschaft in Leipzig:
"Weichet nur," "Zerreisset, zersprenget" and "Geschwinde, ihr wirbelnden Winde" are from the 11th year (second part), 1861 (actually 1862), first volume of the series *Kammermusik für Gesang*, edited by Wilhelm Rust.
"Was mir behagt," "Schweigt stille" and "Mer hahn" are from the 29th year, 1879 (actually 1881), third volume of *Kammermusik für Gesang*, edited by Paul Count Waldersee.

The literal English translation of the texts was prepared specially for the present edition by Stanley Appelbaum.

*International Standard Book Number: 0-486-23934-9*
*Library of Congress Catalog Card Number: 79-56407*

Manufactured in the United States of America
Dover Publications, Inc.
180 Varick Street
New York, N.Y. 10014

# Cantate.
## „Was mir behagt, ist nur die muntre Jagd."

"Was mir behagt" (Hunt Cantata)

12 "Was mir behagt" (Hunt Cantata)

18 "Was mir behagt" (Hunt Cantata)

"Was mir behagt" (Hunt Cantata)

22 "Was mir behagt" (Hunt Cantata)

26 "Was mir behagt" (Hunt Cantata)

"Was mir behagt" (Hunt Cantata)

28 "Was mir behagt" (Hunt Cantata)

"Was mir behagt" (Hunt Cantata)

30 "Was mir behagt" (Hunt Cantata)

"Was mir behagt" (Hunt Cantata)

34 "Was mir behagt" (Hunt Cantata)

36 "Was mir behagt" (Hunt Cantata)

"Was mir behagt" (Hunt Cantata)

"Was mir behagt" (Hunt Cantata)

40 "Was mir behagt" (Hunt Cantata)

# CANTATE.
## „Weichet nur, betrübte Schatten."

"Weichet nur" (Wedding Cantata)

48 "Weichet nur" (Wedding Cantata)

"Weichet nur" (Wedding Cantata)

50 "Weichet nur" (Wedding Cantata)

54 "Weichet nur" (Wedding Cantata)

"Weichet nur" (Wedding Cantata)

# Der zufriedengestellte Aeolus.
## DRAMMA PER MUSICA.
„Zerreisset, zersprenget, zertrümmert die Gruft."

58 "Zerreisset, zersprenget" (Aeolus Appeased)

"Zerreisset, zersprenget" (Aeolus Appeased)

60 "Zerreisset, zersprenget" (Aeolus Appeased)

"Zerreisset, zersprenget" (Aeolus Appeased)

62 "Zerreisset, zersprenget" (Aeolus Appeased)

64 "Zerreisset, zersprenget" (Aeolus Appeased)

66 "Zerreisset, zersprenget" (Aeolus Appeased)

"Zerreisset, zersprenget" (Aeolus Appeased)

68 "Zerreisset, zersprenget" (Aeolus Appeased)

"Zerreisset, zersprenget" (Aeolus Appeased)

70 "Zerreisset, zersprenget" (Aeolus Appeased)

"Zerreisset, zersprenget" (Aeolus Appeased)

"Zerreisset, zersprenget" (Aeolus Appeased)

"Zerreisset, zersprenget" (Aeolus Appeased)

78 "Zerreisset, zersprenget" (Aeolus Appeased)

"Zerreisset, zersprenget" (Aeolus Appeased)

"Zerreisset, zersprenget" (Aeolus Appeased)

82 "Zerreisset, zersprenget" (Aeolus Appeased)

"Zerreisset, zersprenget" (Aeolus Appeased)

84 "Zerreisset, zersprenget" (Aeolus Appeased)

86 "Zerreisset, zersprenget" (Aeolus Appeased)

88 "Zerreisset, zersprenget" (Aeolus Appeased)

"Zerreisset, zersprenget" (Aeolus Appeased)

90 "Zerreisset, zersprenget" (Aeolus Appeased)

"Zerreisset, zersprenget" (Aeolus Appeased)

"Zerreisset, zersprenget" (Aeolus Appeased)

94 "Zerreisset, zersprenget" (Aeolus Appeased)

"Zerreisset, zersprenget" (Aeolus Appeased)

98 "Zerreisset, zersprenget" (Aeolus Appeased)

"Zerreisset, zersprenget" (Aeolus Appeased)

104 "Zerreisset, zersprenget" (Aeolus Appeased)

106 "Zerreisset, zersprenget" (Aeolus Appeased)

"Zerreisset, zersprenget" (Aeolus Appeased)

110 "Zerreisset, zersprenget" (Aeolus Appeased)

112 "Zerreisset, zersprenget" (Aeolus Appeased)

114 "Zerreisset, zersprenget" (Aeolus Appeased)

116 "Zerreisset, zersprenget" (Aeolus Appeased)

120 "Zerreisset, zersprenget" (Aeolus Appeased)

122 "Zerreisset, zersprenget" (Aeolus Appeased)

124 "Zerreisset, zersprenget" (Aeolus Appeased)

126 "Zerreisset, zersprenget" (Aeolus Appeased)

"Zerreisset, zersprenget" (Aeolus Appeased)

130 "Zerreisset, zersprenget" (Aeolus Appeased)

"Zerreisset, zersprenget" (Aeolus Appeased)

134 "Zerreisset, zersprenget" (Aeolus Appeased)

"Zerreisset, zersprenget" (Aeolus Appeased)

136 "Zerreisset, zersprenget" (Aeolus Appeased)

"Zerreisset, zersprenget" (Aeolus Appeased)

138 "Zerreisset, zersprenget" (Aeolus Appeased)

"Zerreisset, zersprenget" (Aeolus Appeased)

140 "Zerreisset, zersprenget" (Aeolus Appeased)

"Zerreisset, zersprenget" (Aeolus Appeased)

142 "Zerreisset, zersprenget" (Aeolus Appeased)

144 "Zerreisset, zersprenget" (Aeolus Appeased)

"Zerreisset, zersprenget" (Aeolus Appeased)

146 "Zerreisset, zersprenget" (Aeolus Appeased)

# Der Streit zwischen Phoebus und Pan.
## DRAMMA PER MUSICA.
„Geschwinde, ihr wirbelnden Winde."

148 "Geschwinde" (Phoebus and Pan)

"Geschwinde" (Phoebus and Pan)

150 "Geschwinde" (Phoebus and Pan)

"Geschwinde" (Phoebus and Pan)

"Geschwinde" (Phoebus and Pan)

154 "Geschwinde" (Phoebus and Pan)

"Geschwinde" (Phoebus and Pan)

156 "Geschwinde" (Phoebus and Pan)

158 "Geschwinde" (Phoebus and Pan)

"Geschwinde" (Phoebus and Pan)

160 "Geschwinde" (Phoebus and Pan)

"Geschwinde" (Phoebus and Pan)

162 "Geschwinde" (Phoebus and Pan)

"Geschwinde" (Phoebus and Pan)

166 "Geschwinde" (Phoebus and Pan)

168 "Geschwinde" (Phoebus and Pan)

174 "Geschwinde" (Phoebus and Pan)

176 "Geschwinde" (Phoebus and Pan)

"Geschwinde" (Phoebus and Pan)

178 "Geschwinde" (Phoebus and Pan)

"Geschwinde" (Phoebus and Pan)

184 "Geschwinde" (Phoebus and Pan)

"Geschwinde" (Phoebus and Pan)

"Geschwinde" (Phoebus and Pan)

"Geschwinde" (Phoebus and Pan)

194 "Geschwinde" (Phoebus and Pan)

"Geschwinde" (Phoebus and Pan)

196 "Geschwinde" (Phoebus and Pan)

200 "Geschwinde" (Phoebus and Pan)

202 "Geschwinde" (Phoebus and Pan)

204 "Geschwinde" (Phoebus and Pan)

206 "Geschwinde" (Phoebus and Pan)

"Geschwinde" (Phoebus and Pan)

208 "Geschwinde" (Phoebus and Pan)

"Geschwinde" (Phoebus and Pan)

212 "Geschwinde" (Phoebus and Pan)

214 "Geschwinde" (Phoebus and Pan)

"Geschwinde" (Phoebus and Pan)

# Cantate.
## „Schweigt stille, plaudert nicht."

"Schweigt stille" (Coffee Cantata)

218 "Schweigt stille" (Coffee Cantata)

220 "Schweigt stille" (Coffee Cantata)

"Schweigt stille" (Coffee Cantata)

222 "Schweigt stille" (Coffee Cantata)

"Schweigt stille" (Coffee Cantata)

228 "Schweigt stille" (Coffee Cantata)

"Schweigt stille" (Coffee Cantata)

"Schweigt stille" (Coffee Cantata)

234 "Schweigt stille" (Coffee Cantata)

"Schweigt stille" (Coffee Cantata)

"Schweigt stille" (Coffee Cantata)

242  "Schweigt stille" (Coffee Cantata)

244 "Schweigt stille" (Coffee Cantata)

"Schweigt stille" (Coffee Cantata)

248 "Schweigt stille" (Coffee Cantata)

# Cantate.
## „Mer hahn en neue Oberkeet."

250 "Mer hahn" (Peasant Cantata)

"Mer hahn" (Peasant Cantata)

252 "Mer hahn" (Peasant Cantata)

254 "Mer hahn" (Peasant Cantata)

256 "Mer hahn" (Peasant Cantata)

262 "Mer hahn" (Peasant Cantata)

264 "Mer hahn" (Peasant Cantata)

270 "Mer hahn" (Peasant Cantata)

276 "Mer hahn" (Peasant Cantata)

"Mer hahn" (Peasant Cantata)

280 "Mer hahn" (Peasant Cantata)

# TRANSLATION OF TEXTS

## Was mir behagt, ist nur die muntre Jagd

RECITATIVE (DIANA):
Was mir behagt,
ist nur die muntre Jagd!
Eh' noch Aurora pranget,
eh' sie sich an den Himmel wagt,
hat dieser Pfeil schon angenehme Beut' erlanget.

ARIA (DIANA):
Jagen ist die Lust der Götter,
Jagen steht den Helden an!
Weichet, meiner Nymphen Spötter,
weichet von Dianen Bahn!

RECITATIVE (ENDYMION):
Wie, schönste Göttin, wie? Kennst du
nicht mehr dein vormals halbes Leben?
Hast du nicht dem Endymion in seiner sanften Ruh'
so manchen Zuckerkuss gegeben?
Bist du dann, Schönste, nu,
von Liebesbanden frei
und folgest nur der Jägerei?

ARIA (ENDYMION):
Willst du dich nicht mehr ergetzen
an den Netzen,
die dir Amor legt?
Wo man auch, wenn man gefangen,
nach Verlangen,
Lust und Lieb' in Banden pflegt.

RECITATIVE (DIANA & ENDYMION):
(DIA.:) Ich liebe dich zwar noch!
Jedoch
ist heut' ein hohes Licht erschienen,
das ich vor allem muss
mit meinem Liebeskuss
empfangen und bedienen!
Der theure Christian,*
der Wälder Pan,
kann in erwünschtem Wohlergehen
sein hohes Ursprungs-Fest itzt sehen.
(END.:) So gönne nur, Diana, dass ich mich mit dir itzund verbinde,
und an "ein Freuden-Opfer" zünde.
(BOTH:) Ja! Wir tragen unsre Flammen
mit Wunsch und Freuden itzt zusammen.

RECITATIVE (PAN):
Ich, der ich sonst ein Gott in diesen Feldern bin,
ich lege meinen Schäfer-Stab vor Christian's Regierungs-Scepter hin!
Weil der durchlauchte Pan das Land so glücklich machet,
dass Wald und Feld, und Alles lebt und lachet!

ARIA (PAN):
Ein Fürst ist seines Landes Pan!
Gleichwie der Körper ohne Seele
nicht leben, noch sich regen kann;
so ist das Land die Todtenhöhle,
das sonder Haupt und Fürsten ist,
und so das beste Theil vermisst.

RECITATIVE (PALES):
Soll dann der Pales Opfer hier das letzte sein?
Nein! nein!
Ich will die Pflicht auch niederlegen,
und da das ganze Land vom Vivat schallt, auch dieses schöne Feld
zu Ehren unserm Sachsen-Held,
zur Freud' und Lust bewegen!

ARIA (PALES):
Schafe können sicher weiden, wo ein guter Hirte wacht.
Wo Regenten wohl regieren,
kann man Ruh' und Frieden spüren,
und was Länder glücklich macht.

RECITATIVE (DIANA):
So stimmt mit ein,
und lasst des Tages Lust vollkommen sein!

What I enjoy
is just the merry hunt!
Even before Dawn rises in splendor,
before she dares to appear in the sky,
my arrow has already struck down pleasing game.

Hunting is the pleasure of the gods,
hunting is befitting to heroes!
Make way, you that mock at my nymphs,
make way at Diana's approach!

What, fairest goddess, what? Do you
no longer recognize what was once half your life?
Haven't you given many a sugared kiss
to Endymion as he gently slept?
Are you then, fairest one, now
liberated from the bonds of love
and engaged only in the hunt?

Do you no longer wish to take delight
in the nets
that Love spreads for you? —
in which, even when you are captured,
as much as you desire
you can nurture love and joy in your bonds.

It's true that I still love you!
And yet
a noble light has appeared today,
whom I must above all
receive and serve
with my kiss of love!
Dear Christian,
the Pan of the forests,
can, with desirable well-being,
now see the lofty celebration of his origins.
Then, allow me, Diana, to join you now

in lighting "a sacrifice of joy."
Yes! We now bring together our flames
with good wishes and joy.

I, usually a god in these fields,
lay down my shepherd's crook before Christian's scepter of office!
Because this illustrious Pan makes the land so happy
that forest, field and everything live and laugh!

A prince is a Pan to his country!
Just as the body without a soul
cannot live or move,
so a country is a mortuary cavern
if it is without a head and a prince
and thus lacks its finest part.

Shall Pales' offering then be the last one here?
No, no!
I want to do my duty, too,
and since the whole land resounds with hurrahs, this lovely field as well,
in honor of our Saxon hero,
I shall infuse with joy and pleasure!

Sheep may safely graze where a good shepherd stands guard.
Where rulers rule well,
You can perceive peace and quiet
And all that makes countries happy.

Then join your voices to ours,
and let the day's pleasure be complete!

*Throughout the cantata, the score gives "Ernst August" as an alternate for "Christian" because Bach later revived the piece to honor the Saxon prince of that name.

CHORUS:
Lebe, Sonne dieser Erden,
weil Diana bei der Nacht
an der Burg des Himmels wacht,
weil die Wälder grünen werden.

DUET (DIANA & ENDYMION):
Entzücket uns beide,
ihr Strahlen der Freude,
und zieret den Himmel mit Demant-Geschmeide,
Fürst Christian weide
auf lieblichsten Rosen, befreiet vom Leide.

ARIA (PALES):
Weil die wollenreichen Heerden
durch dies weitgepries'ne Feld
lustig ausgetrieben werden,
lebe dieser Sachsen-Held.

ARIA (PAN):
Ihr Felder und Auen,
lasst grünend euch schauen,
ruft Vivat itzt zu.
Es lebe der Herzog in Segen und Ruh'.

CHORUS:
Ihr lieblichste Blicke, ihr freudige Stunden,
euch bleibe das Glücke auf ewig verbunden!
Euch kröne der Himmel mit süssester Lust!
Fürst Christian lebe! Ihm bleibe bewusst,
was Herzen vergnüget,
was Trauern besieget!

## Weichet nur, betrübte Schatten

Weichet nur, betrübte Schatten,
Frost und Winde, geht zur Ruh'!
Florens Lust
will der Brust
nichts als frohes Glück verstatten,
denn sie träget Blumen zu.

RECITATIVE:
Die Welt wird wieder neu,
auf Bergen und in Gründen
will sich die Anmuth doppelt schön verbinden,
der Tag ist von der Kälte frei.

ARIA:
Phöbus eilt mit schnellen Pferden
durch die neugeborne Welt.
Ja, weil sie ihm wohlgefällt,
will er selbst ein Buhler werden.

RECITATIVE:
D'rum sucht auch Amor sein Vergnügen,
wenn Purpur in den Wiesen lacht,
wenn Florens Pracht
sich herrlich macht,
und wenn in seinem Reich,
den schönen Blumen gleich,
auch Herzen feurig siegen.

ARIA:
Wenn die Frühlingslüfte streichen
und durch bunte Felder wehn,
pflegt auch Amor auszuschleichen,
um nach seinem Schmuck zu sehn;
welcher, glaubt man, dieser ist:
dass ein Herz das andre küsst.

RECITATIVE:
Und dieses ist das Glücke,
dass durch ein hohes Gunstgeschicke
zwei Seelen einen Schmuck erlanget,
an dem viel Heil und Segen pranget.

ARIA:
Sich üben
im lieben,
in Scherzen
sich herzen
ist besser als Florens vergängliche Lust.
Hier quellen
die Wellen,
hier lachen
und wachen
die siegenden Palmen auf Lippen und Brust.

RECITATIVE:
So sei das Band der keuschen Liebe,
verlobte Zwei,
vom Unbestand des Wechsels frei.
Kein jäher Fall,
noch Donnerknall
erschrecke die verliebten Triebe!

GAVOTTE:
Sehet in Zufriedenheit
tausend helle Wohlfahrtstage,
dass bald bei der Folgezeit
eure Liebe Blumen trage.

Live, O sun of this earth,
as long as Diana at night
stands guard in the fortress of Heaven,
as long as the forests become green.

Delight us both,
beams of joy,
and adorn the sky with diamond jewels;
may Prince Christian loll
on loveliest roses, freed from sorrow.

As long as the wool-rich flocks
are merrily driven out to pasture
through this far-renowned field,
so long may this Saxon hero live.

You fields and meadows,
let us see you clad in green;
shout hurrah now.
Long live the Duke with blessings and peace.

You lovely glances, you joyful hours,
may happiness forever be associated with you!
May Heaven crown you with sweetest pleasure!
Long live Prince Christian! May he remain conscious
of all that delights the heart
and conquers sadness!

Depart, melancholy shadows;
frost and winds, go to rest!
Flora's pleasure
wants to grant the heart
nothing but merry happiness,
for she is bringing flowers.

The world becomes new again;
on mountains and in valleys
gracefulness becomes doubly graceful;
the day is free of cold.

Phoebus hastens with swift horses
through the new-born world.
Yes, because he likes it
he wants to become a lover himself.

Therefore Love, too, seeks for pleasure
when purple laughs in the meadows,
when Flora's splendor
becomes magnificent,
and when in his (Love's) kingdom,
like beautiful flowers,
hearts, too, blaze and conquer.

When spring breezes caress you
and waft through the colorful fields,
Love, too, is wont to sneak out
and look after his adornment,
which, it is believed, is this:
that one heart kisses another.

And this is happiness,
that through a lofty, favorable fate
two souls obtain an adornment
on which well-being and many blessings gleam.

To practice
loving,
to hug and kiss
in sport,
is better than Flora's perishable pleasure.
Here fountains
splash,
here victorious palms laugh
and keep vigil
on lips and heart.

So let the bond of chaste love,
betrothed pair,
be free of uncertainty and change.
May no sudden accident
or thunderclap
alarm your loving caresses!

May you see in contentment
a thousand bright days of well-being,
so that in the near future
your love will bear blossoms.

## Zerreisset, zerspr

CHORUS OF THE WINDS:
Zerreisset, zersprenget, zertrümmert die Gruft,
die unserm Wüthen Gränze giebt.
Durchbrechet die Luft,
dass selber die Sonne zur Finsterniss werde;
durchschneidet die Fluthen, durchwühlet die Erde,
dass sich der Himmel selbst betrübt!

RECITATIVE (AEOLUS):
Ja! ja! die Stunden sind nunmehro nah',
dass ich euch treuen Unterthanen
den Weg aus eurer Einsamkeit,
nach bald geschloss'ner Sommerszeit,
zur Freiheit werde bahnen.
Ich geb' euch Macht,
vom Abend bis zum Morgen, vom Mittag bis zur
    Mitternacht
mit eurer Wuth zu rasen,
die Blumen, Blätter, Klee,
mit Kälte, Frost und Schnee
entsetzlich anzublasen.
Ich geb' euch Macht, die Cedern umzuschmeissen,
und Bergegipfel aufzureissen.
Ich geb' euch Macht, die ungestümen Meeresfluthen
durch euren Nachdruck zu erhöh'n,
dass das Gestirne wird vermuthen,
ihr Feuer soll durch euch verlöschend untergehn.

ARIA (AEOLUS):
Wie will ich lustig lachen,
wenn Alles durcheinander geht!
Wenn selbst der Fels nicht sicher steht
und wenn die Dächer krachen!

RECITATIVE (ZEPHYR):
Gefürcht'ter Aeolus,
dem ich im Schoosse sonsten liege,
und deine Ruh' vergnüge,
lass deinen harten Schluss
mich doch nicht allzu früh erschrecken;
verziehe, lass in dir,
aus Gunst zu mir,
ein Mitleid noch erwecken.

ARIA (ZEPHYR):
Frische Schatten, meine Freude,
sehet, wie ich schmerzlich scheide,
kommt, bedauert meine Schmach.
Windet euch, verwaisten Zweige,
ach! ich schweige,
sehet mir nur jammernd nach.

RECITATIVE (AEOLUS):
Beinahe wirst du mich bewegen.
Wie? seh' ich nicht Pomona hier,
und, wo mir recht, die Pallas auch bei ihr?
Sagt, Werthe, sagt, was fordert ihr von mir?
Euch ist gewiss sehr viel daran gelegen.

ARIA (POMONA):
Können nicht die rothen Wangen,
womit meine Früchte prangen,
dein ergrimmtes Herze fangen,
ach, so sage, kannst du sehn,
wie die Blätter von den Zweigen
sich betrübt zur Erde beugen
um ihr Elend abzuneigen,
das an ihnen soll geschehn.

RECITATIVE (POMONA & PALLAS):
(POM.:) So willst du, grimm'ger Aeolus,
gleich wie ein Fels und Stein
bei meinen Bitten sein?
(PAL.:) Wohlan! ich will und muss
auch meine Seufzer wagen,
vielleicht wird mir,
was er, Pomona, dir
stillschweigend abgeschlagen,
von ihm gewährt.
(BOTH:) Wohl! wenn er gegen mich (Dich) sich
    gütiger erklärt.

ARIA (PALLAS):
Angenehmer Zephyrus,
dein von Bisam reicher Kuss
und dein lauschend Kühlen
soll auf meinen Höhen spielen.
Grosser König, Aeolus,
sage doch dem Zephyrus,
dass sein Bisamreicher Kuss
und sein lauschend Kühlen
soll auf meinen Höhen spielen.

RECITATIVE (PALLAS & AEOLUS):
(PAL.:) Mein Aeolus, ach! störe nicht die
    Fröhlichkeiten,
weil meiner Musen Helicon
ein Fest, ein' angenehme Feier
auf seinen Gipfeln angestellt.
(AEO.:) So sage mir: warum denn dir besonders

ümmert die Gruft

Rip apart, break open, demolish the cave
that sets limit to our raging.
Pierce the air,
so that the sun itself becomes dark;
cut through the waves, bore through the earth,
so that Heaven itself becomes sad!

Yes, yes! the time is now near
when for you, my loyal subjects,
I will prepare a way out of your solitude,
now that summer is nearly over,
and restore your freedom.
I empower you,
from evening to morning, from noon to midnight,
to rage in your fury,
to blow horribly
on flowers, leaves and clover
with cold, frost and snow.
I empower you to knock down the cedars
and to rip open mountaintops.
I empower you to raise the stormy ocean waves
with your pressure,
so that the heavenly bodies will assume
that through you their fires will be put out and
    perish.

How merrily I will laugh
when everything becomes chaotic!
When even crags become insecure
and roofs break in!

Greatly feared Aeolus,
in whose lap I often lie
adding pleasure to your repose,
don't let your rigorous decision
frighten me too soon;
wait a bit, allow yourself
out of kindness to me
to feel a touch of pity.

Cool shadows, my joy,
see how painfully I depart;
come, lament for my disgrace.
Twist, you orphaned branches –
ah, I will be silent –
just watch me sorrowfully as I leave.

If you go on, you might persuade me.
What? Don't I see Pomona here,
and, if I'm not mistaken, Pallas along with her?
Tell me, good ladies, what do you ask of me?
You certainly are quite concerned about it.

If the red cheeks
that make my fruits beautiful
fail to touch your angered heart,
ah, then tell me, can you bear to see
how the leaves on the branches
sadly bend to the ground
to avert the misery
that is to overtake them?

So then, irate Aeolus, you will
remain as hard as a rock
despite my entreaties?
Well, then, I must and will
make bold and see what my sighs will do;
perhaps
what he silently refused
to you, Pomona,
he will grant me.
I hope he will prove kinder to me (you).

Pleasant Zephyr,
let your kiss laden with musk
and your listening coolness
play upon my mountain heights.
Great king, Aeolus,
please tell Zephyr
to let his musk-laden kiss
and his listening coolness
play upon my mountain heights.

My Aeolus, ah, don't upset the festivities,
because the Helicon of my Muses
has arranged on its peaks
a party, a pleasant celebration.
Then tell me, why is this day so especially dear

dieser Tag so theuer,
so werth und heilig fällt? –
O Nachtheil und Verdruss! soll ich denn eines
    Weibes Willen
in meinem Regiment erfüllen? –
(PAL.:) Mein Müller, mein August,
der Pierinnen Freud' und Lust
und mein geliebter Sohn
erlebet die vergnügten Zeiten,
da ihm die Ewigkeit
sein weiser Name prophezeit.
(AEO.:) Wohlan! ich lasse mich bezwingen,
euer Wunsch soll euch gelingen.

ARIA (AEOLUS):
Zurücke, geflügelten Winde,
besänftiget euch.
Doch wehet ihr gleich,
so weht doch jetzund, nur gelinde.

RECITATIVE (PALLAS, POMONA & ZEPHYR):
(PAL.:) Was Lust! (POM.:) Was Freude! (ZEP.:)
    Welch Vergnügen!
(ALL:) entstehet in der Brust,
dass sich nach unsrer Lust
die Wünsche müssen fügen.
(ZEP.:) So kann ich mich bei grünen Zweigen
noch fernerhin vergnügt bezeigen.
(POM.:) So seh' ich mein Ergötzen
an meinen reifen Schätzen.
(PAL.:) So richt' ich in vergnügter Ruh'
meines August's Lustmahl zu.
(POM. & ZEP.:) Wir sind zu deiner Fröhlichkeit
mit gleicher Lust bereit.

DUET (POMONA & ZEPHYR):
(POM.:) Zweig' und Aeste
zollen dir zu deinem Feste
ihrer Gaben Ueberfluss.
(ZEP.:) Und mein Scherzen soll und muss,
deinen August zu verehren,
dieses Tages Lust vermehren.
(BOTH:) Ich bringe dir Früchte (Ich bringe mein
    Lispeln) mit Freuden herbei,
dass Alles zum Scherzen vollkommener sei.

RECITATIVE (PALLAS):
Ja! ja! ich lad' euch selbst zu dieser Feier ein:
erhebet euch zu meinen Spitzen,
wo schon die Musen freudig sein,
und ganz entbrannt vor Eifer sitzen.
Auf! lasset uns, indem wir eilen,
die Luft mit frohen Wünschen theilen.

CHORUS:
Vivat August, August vivat, sei beglückt
    gelehrter Mann!
Dein Vergnügen müsse blühen,
dass dein Lehren, dein Bemühen
möge solche Pflanzen ziehen,
womit ein Land sich einstens schmücken kann.

## Geschwinde, ihr wirbelnden Winde

Geschwinde, geschwinde,
ihr wirbelnden Winde,
auf einmal zusammen zur Höhle hinein!
Dass das Hin- und Wiederschallen
selbst dem Echo mag gefallen,
und den Lüften lieblich sein.

RECITATIVE (PHOEBUS, PAN & MOMUS):
(PHO.:) Und du bist doch so unverschämt und frei,
mir in das Angesicht zu sagen,
dass dein Gesang
viel herrlicher als meiner sei?
(PAN:) Wie kannst du doch so lange fragen?
Der ganze Wald bewundert meinen Klang;
das Nymphen-Chor,
das mein von mir erfund'nes Rohr
von sieben wohlgesetzten Stufen
zum Tanzen öfters aufgerufen,
wird dir von selbsten zugestehn:
Pan singt vor allen andern schön.
(PHO.:) Vor Nymphen bist du recht;
allein, die Götter zu vergnügen,
ist deine Flöte viel zu schlecht.
(PAN:) Sobald mein Ton die Luft erfüllt,
so hüpfen die Berge, so tanzet das Wild,
so müssen sich die Zweige biegen,
und unter denen Sternen
geht ein entzücktes Springen für:
die Vögel setzen sich zu mir
und wollen von mir singen lernen.
(MOM.:) Ei! hört mir doch den Pan,
den grossen Meister-Sänger an!

ARIA (MOMUS):
Patron, das macht der Wind!
Dass man prahlt und hat kein Geld,
das macht der Wind!

to you,
so dignified and sacred? –
O injury and vexation! Am I then to fulfill a
    woman's wish
in the management of my own affairs? –
My Müller, my August,
the joy and pleasure of the Muses
and my beloved son,
is experiencing a pleasing hour,
since his reputation for wisdom
prophesies eternal fame for him.
All right! I yield,
your wish will be granted.

Back, winged winds,
calm down.
But if you do blow,
blow only very gently now.

What pleasure! What joy! What delight

arises in our heart,
because according to our desire
our wishes must come true.
Then, I can continue to take delight
among the green branches.
Then, I see my enjoyment
of my ripe treasures.
Then, in pleasant calm
I can prepare my August's banquet.
We are ready for your festivity
with equal pleasure.

Branches and boughs
pay tribute to your celebration
with the abundance of their gifts.
And my frolicking must and will,
in honor of your August,
increase the pleasure of this day.
I bring you fruits (I bring my whispering) with
    joy,
so that all our sporting will be more complete.

Yes, yes! I myself invite you to this celebration:
Go up to my mountain summits,
where the Muses, already joyful,
are seated in a frenzy of eagerness.
Come! Let us, as we hasten there,
cleave the air with joyous wishes.

Long live August, long live August, be happy,
    learned man!
May your enjoyment blossom,
may your teaching and your efforts
raise such fine plants
that in time to come they will be the ornament of
    our land.

Quickly, quickly,
you whirling winds,
enter your cave together at once,
so that the tones resounding back and forth
may please the very echo
and be gratifying to the breezes.

And thus you are so impudent and bold
as to tell me in my face
that your singing
is much more splendid than mine?
How can you keep on doubting it?
The whole forest admires my music;
the chorus of nymphs
whom my pipes – my own invention,
made of seven gradated lengths –
have often summoned to the dance,
will readily admit to you
that Pan sings more beautifully than anyone else.
You're good enough for nymphs,
but to satisfy the gods
your flute is much too primitive.
As soon as my tones fill the air,
the mountains hop, the wild animals dance,
all the branches are compelled to bend,
and among the stars
a rapturous leaping breaks out;
the birds fly down near me
and want to learn singing from me.
Ho! Just listen to Pan,
the great master singer!

Sir, that's just bluster!
When people swagger but have no money,
that's just bluster!

dass man das für Wahrheit hält,
was nur in die Augen fällt,
das macht der Wind!
Dass die Thoren weise sind,
das macht der Wind!
dass das Glücke selber blind,
das macht der Wind!

RECITATIVE (MERCURY, PHOEBUS & PAN):
(MER.:) Was braucht ihr euch zu zanken?
Ihr weichet doch einander nicht.
Nach meinen wenigen Gedanken,
so wähle sich ein Jeder einen Mann,
der zwischen euch das Urtheil spricht;
lasst sehn, wer fällt euch ein?
(PHO.:) Der Tmolus soll mein Richter sein,
(PAN:) und Mydas sei auf meiner Seite.
(MER.:) So tretet her, ihr lieben Leute,
hört alles fleissig an,
und merket, wer das Beste kann.

ARIA (PHOEBUS):
Mit Verlangen
drück' ich deine zarten Wangen,
holder, schöner Hyacinth.
Und dein' Augen küss' ich gerne,
weil sie meine Morgensterne
und der Seele Sonne sind.

RECITATIVE (MOMUS & PAN):
(MOM.:) Pan, rücke deine Kehle nun
in wohlgestimmte Falten.
(PAN:) Ich will mein Bestes thun,
und mich noch herrlicher, als Phoebus, halten.

ARIA (PAN):
Zu Tanze, zu Sprunge, so wackelt das Herz.
Wenn der Ton zu mühsam klingt,
und der Mund gebunden singt,
so erweckt es keinen Scherz.

RECITATIVE (MERCURY & TMOLUS):
(MER.:) Nunmehro Richter her!
(TMO.:) Das Urtheil fällt mir gar nicht schwer,
die Wahrheit wird es selber sagen,
das Phoebus hier den Preis davongetragen.
Pan singet für den Wald,
die Nymphen kann er wohl ergötzen;
jedoch so schön als Phoebus' Klang erschallt,
ist seine Flöte nicht zu schätzen.

ARIA (TMOLUS):
Phoebus, deine Melodei hat die Anmuth selbst geboren.
Aber, wer die Kunst versteht,
wie dein Ton verwundernd geht,
wird dabei aus sich verloren.

RECITATIVE (PAN & MIDAS):
(PAN:) Komm, Mydas, sage du nun an,
was ich gethan.
(MID.:) Ach Pan! wie hast du mich gestärkt,
dein Lied hat mir so wohl geklungen,
dass ich es mir auf einmal gleich gemerkt.
Nun geh' ich hier im Grünen auf und nieder
und lehr' es denen Bäumen wieder.
Der Phoebus macht es gar zu bunt;
allein, dein allerliebster Mund
sang leicht und ungezwungen.

ARIA (MIDAS):
Pan ist Meister, lasst ihn gehn.
Phoebus hat den Spiel verloren,
denn nach meinen beiden Ohren
singt er unvergleichlich schön.

RECITATIVE (MOMUS, MERCURY, TMOLUS, PHOEBUS, MIDAS & PAN):
(MOM.:) Wie, Mydas, bist du toll?
(MER.:) Wer hat dir den Verstand verrückt?
(TMO.:) Das dacht' ich wohl,
dass du so ungeschickt!
(PHO.:) Sprich, was ich mit dir machen soll?
verkehr' ich dich in Raben,
soll ich dich schinden oder schaben?
(MID.:) Ach! plaget mich doch nicht so sehre,
es fiel mir ja also in mein Gehöre.
(PHO.:) Sieh' da, so sollst du Eselsohren haben.
(MER.:) Das ist der Lohn der tollen Ehrbegierigkeit.
(PAN:) Ei! warum hast du diesen Streit
auf leichte Schultern übernommen?
(MID.:) Wie ist mir die Commission so schlecht bekommen!

ARIA (MERCURY):
Aufgeblas'ne Hitze,
aber wenig Grütze
kriegt die Schellenmütze
endlich aufgesetzt.
Wer das Schiffen nicht versteht
und doch an das Ruder geht,
ertrinket mit Schaden und Schanden zuletzt.

When people accept as the truth
what is merely an outward appearance,
that's just bluster!
When fools act wise,
that's just bluster!
If Fortune itself is blind,
that's just bluster!

Why do you need to scrap?
You're not going to convince each other.
In my humble opinion,
each of you should choose a man
to pass judgment between you.
Let's see, who comes to your mind?
Tmolus shall be the judge I name.
And for my part, let it be Midas.
So then, step this way, dear people,
listen to everything attentively
and take note of who does the best.

With longing
I touch your tender face,
fair, beautiful Hyacinth.
And I love to kiss your eyes
because they are my morning stars
and the sun of my soul.

Pan, now get your gullet
into good shape for singing.
I'll do my best
and come out much finer than Phoebus.

Dancing, jumping, that's what makes your heart leap.
When music is too difficult
and singers are too stodgy,
you get no fun out of it.

Judges, this way now!
I don't find the decision hard at all,
it's just a matter of the simple truth
that Phoebus has walked off with the prize here.
Pan's singing is for the woods;
he can no doubt entertain the nymphs;
but Phoebus' music sounded so beautiful
that Pan's flute can't be compared with it.

Phoebus, grace itself gave birth to your melody.
The man who understands art
finds your tones so astonishing
that he is beside himself when he hears them.

Come, Midas now you tell
what I have done.
Oh, Pan! How you have invigorated me!
Your song sounded so good to me
that I learned it immediately.
Now I walk to and fro outside here
and teach it in turn to the trees.
Phoebus' song was far too overdone,
but your most pleasing lips
sang easily and without constraint.

Pan is the master, let him alone.
Phoebus has lost the contest
because to my two ears
he (Pan) sings incomparably well.

What, Midas, are you crazy?
Who has deprived you of your senses?
I suspected
that you were as gauche as this!
Tell me, what should I do to to you?
Shall I turn you into a raven?
Shall I flay you or grate you?
Oh! don't torture me that much;
it just happened to please my ear.
That's it! You shall have donkey's ears.
Such is the reward of mad ambition.
Oh, why did you take this quarrel
so lightly?
How badly this task turned out for me!

Puffed-up passion,
combined with a lack of common sense,
finally winds up
wearing the dunce cap.
Those who don't know how to handle boats
but insist on rowing
end up drowning to their distress and shame.

RECITATIVE (MOMUS):
Du guter Mydas, geh' nun hin
und lege dich in deinem Walde nieder,
doch tröste dich in deinem Sinn,
du hast noch mehr dergleichen Brüder.
Der Unverstand und Unvernunft
will jetzt der Weisheit Nachbar sein,
man urtheilt in den Tag hinein,
und die so thun, gehören all' in deine Zunft.
Ergreife, Phoebus, nun die Leyer wieder,
es ist nichts Lieblichers, als deine Lieder.

Labt das Herz, ihr holden Saiten, stimmet
Kunst und Anmuth an.
Lasst euch meistern, lasst euch höhnen,
sind doch euren süssen Tönen
selbst die Götter zugethan.

## Schweigt

RECITATIVE (TENOR):
Schweigt stille, plaudert nicht,
und höret, was jetzund geschicht:
Da kömmt Herr Schlendrian
mit seiner Tochter, Lieschen, her;
er brummt ja wie ein Zeidel-Bär;
hört selber, was sie ihm gethan!

ARIA (SCHLENDRIAN):
Hat man nicht mit seinen Kindern
hunderttausend Hudelei!
Was ich immer alle Tage
meiner Tochter Lieschen sage,
gehet ohne Frucht vorbei!

RECITATIVE (SCHLENDRIAN & LIESCHEN):
(SCH.:) Du böses Kind, du loses Mädchen,
ach! wenn erlang' ich meinen Zweck:
thu' mir den Coffee weg!
(LIE.:) Herr Vater, seid doch nicht so scharf!
Wenn ich des Tages nicht dreimal
mein Schälchen Coffee trinken darf,
so werd' ich ja zu meiner Qual
wie ein verdorrtes Ziegen-Brätchen.

ARIA (LIESCHEN):
Ei! wie schmeckt der Coffee süsse,
lieblicher als tausend Küsse,
milder als Muscatenwein.
Coffee muss ich haben;
und wenn Jemand will mich laben,
ach, so schenkt mir Coffee ein!

RECITATIVE (SCHLENDRIAN & LIESCHEN):
(SCH.:) Wenn du mir nicht den Coffee läss'st,
so sollst du auf kein Hochzeitfest,
auch nicht spazieren geh'n. (LIE.:) Ach ja!
Nur lasset mir den Coffee da!
(SCH.:) Da hab' ich nun den kleinen Affen!
Ich will dir keinen Fischbein-Rock nach
     jetz'ger Weite schaffen.
(LIE.:) Ich kann mich leicht dazu versteh'n.
(SCH.:) Du sollst nicht an das Fenster treten
und Keinen seh'n vorübergeh'n.
(LIE.:) Auch dieses. Doch seid nur gebeten
und lasset mir den Coffee steh'n.
(SCH.:) Du sollst auch nicht von meiner Hand
ein silbern oder gold'nes Band
auf deine Haube kriegen.
(LIE.:) Ja, ja! Nur lasst mir mein Vergnügen.
(SCH.:) Du loses Lieschen du,
so giebst du mir denn Alles zu?

ARIA (SCHLENDRIAN):
Mädchen, die von harten Sinnen,
sind nicht leichte zu gewinnen,
Doch trifft man den rechten Ort:
o! so kömmt man glücklich fort.

RECITATIVE (SCHLENDRIAN & LIESCHEN):
(SCH.:) Nun folge, was dein Vater spricht.
(LIE.:) In Allem, nur den Coffee nicht.
(SCH.:) Wohlan! so musst du dich bequemen,
auch niemals einen Mann zu nehmen.
(LIE.:) Ach ja! Herr Vater, einen Mann!
(SCH.:) Ich schwöre, dass es nicht geschicht, ...
(LIE.:) Bis ich den Coffee lassen kann?
Nun! Coffee, bleib' nur immer liegen!
Herr Vater, hört, ich trinke keinen nicht.
(SCH.:) So sollst du endlich einen kriegen.

ARIA (LIESCHEN):
Heute noch,
lieber Vater, thut es doch.
Ach, ein Mann!
wahrlich, dieser steht mir an,
dieser steht mir trefflich an.
Wenn es sich doch balde fügte,
dass ich endlich vor Coffee,
eh' ich noch zu Bette geh',
einen wackern Liebsten kriegte.

Good Midas, now depart
and lie down in your forest,
but be easy in your mind:
you have more brothers of the same kind.
Lack of brains and lack of sense
nowadays want to be side by side with wisdom;
they pass judgment without due reflection;
and all who do so belong to your guild.
Now, Phoebus, take up your lyre again;
nothing is more delightful than your songs.

Refresh our hearts, lovely strings, play artistically
  and gracefully.
You may be censured, you may be scorned,
but the gods themselves
are devoted to your sweet tones.

Be still, don't chatter,
and listen to what will now happen.
Here comes Mr. Schlendrian (Humdrum)
with his daughter Lieschen;
he's growling like a honey bear;
hear for yourself what she has done to him!

Don't people's children cause them
a hundred thousand vexations!
All that I say every day
to my daughter Lieschen
is ignored and has no result.

You naughty child, you frivolous girl,
oh, when will I achieve my aim?
Give up your coffee!
Father, don't be so severe!
If I am not allowed to drink
my cup of coffee three times a day,
then to my pain
I'll get to be like a dried out goat roast.

Oh, how good coffee tastes,
lovelier than a thousand kisses,
mellower than muscatel.
I must have coffee;
and if someone wants to give me a treat,
he should pour me a cup of coffee!

If you don't stop drinking coffee,
you won't be allowed to go to any weddings,
or even for a walk. – All right!
Just let me keep my coffee!
Now I've got the little monkey!
I won't have a whalebone dress made for you in the
  fullness now in fashion.
I can easily agree to that.
You'll be forbidden to go to the window
and watch people going by.
All right! As long as you relent
and let me go on drinking coffee.
Besides that, you won't get from me
a silver or golden band
for your bonnet.
That's fine! Just leave me my pleasure.
Frivolous Lieschen,
so then you concede everything?

Girls with stubborn minds
aren't easily won over.
But if you hit the right spot,
you come away victorious.

Now pay attention to what your father says.
I obey you on all points, except for the coffee.
Well, then, you must just make up your mind to it
never to get a husband, either.
Oh, yes, Father, a husband!
I swear that it won't happen . . .
until I give up coffee?
Then, goodbye, coffee!
Father, listen, I won't drink any.
Then you'll finally get one (a husband).

Make it today,
Father dear, please do it.
oh, a husband!
That really is what I'd like,
that's exactly what I'd like.
If only it could be arranged soon,
so that finally, in place of coffee,
even before I go to bed,
I could get a brave sweetheart.

RECITATIVE (TENOR):
Nun geht und sucht der alte Schlendrian,
wie er vor seine Tochter Lieschen bald einen
  Mann verschaffen kann;
doch Lieschen streuet heimlich aus:
kein Freier komm' mir in das Haus,
er hab' es mir denn selbst versprochen
und rück' es auch der Ehestiftung ein,
dass mir erlaubet möge sein,
den Coffee, wenn ich will, zu kochen.

ALL THREE SOLOISTS:
Die Katze lässt das Mausen nicht,
die Jungfern bleiben Coffeeschwestern.
Die Mutter liebt den Coffee-Brauch,
die Grossmama trank solchen auch,
wer will nun auf die Töchter lästern.

Now old Schlendrian goes out to see
about getting a husband soon for his daughter
  Lieschen;
but Lieschen spreads the word secretly:
"Let no suitor come to my house
unless he has personally promised me,
and will also add it to the marriage contract,
that I may be allowed
to cook coffee whenever I like."

Cats never give up chasing mice,
and girls always remain coffee fiends.
Mother likes drinking coffee,
Grandma drank it too,
so who can blame our daughters?

## Mer hahn en neue Oberkeet

DUET (UPPER SAXON DIALECT):
Mer hahn en neue Oberkeet
an unsern Kammerherrn.
Ha giebt uns Bier, das steigt in's Heet,
das ist der klare Kern.
Der Pfarr mag immer büse thun;
ihr Speelleut halt euch flink!
Der Kittel wackelt Miecken schun,
das klene luse Ding.

RECITATIVE (SOPRANO & BASS):
(BASS:) Nu, Miecke, gieb dein Guschel immer her;
(SOP.:) Wenn's das alleine wär'.
Ich kenn' dich schon, du Bärenhäuter,
du willst hernach nur immer weiter.
Der neue Herr hat ein sehr scharf Gesicht.
(BASS:) Ach! unser Herr schilt nicht;
er weiss so gut als wir, und auch wohl besser
wie schön ein bisschen Dahlen schmeckt.

ARIA (SOPRANO):
Ach es schmeckt doch gar zu gut,
wenn ein Paar recht freundlich thut;
ei da braust es in dem Ranzen,
als wenn eitel Flöh' und Wanzen
und ein tolles Wespenheer
mit einander zänkisch wär'.

RECITATIVE (BASS):
Der Herr ist gut: Allein der Schösser,
das ist ein Schwefels-Mann,
der wie ein Blitz ein neu Schock strafen kann,
wenn man den Finger kaum in's kalte Wasser
  steckt.

ARIA (BASS):
Ach Herr Schösser, geht nicht gar zu schlimm
mit uns armen Bauersleuten üm.
Schont nur unsre Haut;
fresst ihr gleich das Kraut
wie die Raupen bis zum kahlen Strunk,
habt nur genung.

RECITATIVE (SOPRANO):
Es bleibt dabei,
dass unser Herr der beste sei;
er ist nicht besser abzumalen
und auch mit keinem Hopfensack voll Batzen
  zu bezahlen:

ARIA (SOPRANO):
Unser trefflicher
lieber Kammerherr
ist ein cumpabler Mann,
den Niemand tadeln kann.

RECITATIVE (BASS & SOPRANO):
(BASS:) Er hilft uns allen alt und jung.
Und dir in's Ohr gesprochen:
Ist unser Dorf nicht gut genung
letzt bei der Werbung durchgekrochen?
(SOP.:) Ich weiss wohl noch ein besser Spiel,
der Herr gilt bei der Steuer viel.

ARIA (SOPRANO):
Das ist galant,
es spricht Niemand
von den caducken Schocken,
Niemand red't ein stummes Wort,
Knauthain und Cospuden dort
hat selber Werk am Rocken.

RECITATIVE (BASS):
Und unsre gnäd'ge Frau ist nicht ein prinkel stolz.
Und ist gleich unser eins ein arm und grobes Holz,
so red't sie doch mit uns daher,
als wenn sie unsers Gleichen wär'.
Sie ist recht fromm, recht wirthlich und genau,
  und machte unserm gnäd'gen Herrn
aus einer Fledermaus viel Thaler gern.

We have a new lord of the manor
in our chamberlain.
He gives us beer that goes to our head,
it's the very best stuff.
Let the parson go on frowning at us;
you musicians keep lively!
Mitzi's already shaking her dress,
the frivolous little thing.

Now, Mitzi, pucker up for a kiss.
If that were only all!
I know you well, you idle oaf,
after that you'll want to go further and further.
Our new lord has very good eyesight.
Oh, our lord won't bawl us out;
he knows as well as we do, and maybe even better,
how good a little petting feels.

Oh it sure does feel awful good,
when a couple behave real friendly-like;
say, there's a hubbub in your belly
as if nothing but fleas and bedbugs
and a crazy swarm of wasps
were all spatting with each other.

The lord is good-natured. But his rent collector,
he's a devil out of hell,
who'll fine you a *neu Schock* (sixty groschen) like a flash
if you just stick your finger in cold water.

Oh, mister rent collector, don't treat
us poor peasants so badly.
Spare our hides;
even if you eat the cabbage
down to the bare stem like the caterpillars,
be satisfied at last.

One thing's for certain,
that our lord is the best;
no artist could paint him better than he is,
and you couldn't get a better man for a hop sack
  full of money.

Our wonderful
dear chamberlain
is a sociable man
that no one can find fault with.

He helps all of us, old and young.
And let me whisper this to you:
Didn't our village squeak through pretty well
during the latest recruiting campaign?
I know an even greater advantage:
our lord is in good with the tax commissioners.

It's just dandy,
no one talks
about the overdue tax payments;
no one says a single word;
Knauthain and Cospuden there [two other manors]
are also involved in the same deal.

And our gracious lady isn't a bit proud.
And even though our sort are poor and rough,
she talks to us
as if we were her equals.
She's very pious, very hospitable and a careful house-
  keeper, and for our gracious lord
she could take even a bat and make money out of it.

ARIA (BASS):
Fünfzig Thaler baares Geld
trock'ner Weise zu verschmausen,
ist ein Ding, das harte fällt,
wenn sie uns die Haare zausen,
doch was fort ist, bleibt wohl fort,
kann man doch am andern Ort
alles doppelt wieder sparen;
lass die fünfzig Thaler fahren.

To gobble up fifty talers in cash
just like that
is something that hits you hard
when people are pulling you apart;
but what's gone is gone;
there'll be another opportunity
to save up twice that much again—
forget about the fifty talers.

RECITATIVE (SOPRANO):
Im Ernst ein Wort!
Noch eh' ich dort
an unsre Schenke
und an den Tanz gedenke,
so sollst du erst der Obrigkeit zu Ehren
ein neues Liedchen von mir hören.

To be serious for a moment:
before I
think about the tavern
and the dance,
you shall first hear a new little song of mine
in honor of our master.

ARIA (SOPRANO):
Klein-Zschocher müsse
so zart und süsse
wie lauter Mandelkerne sein.
In unsere Gemeine
zieh' heute ganz alleine
der Überfluss des Segens ein.

Let Klein-Zschocher
be as tender and sweet
as pure almonds.
May abundance of blessings
come this very day
to our community.

RECITATIVE (BASS):
Das ist zu klug vor dich
und nach der Städter Weise;
wir Bauern singen nicht so leise.
Das Stückchen, höre nur, das schicket sich
  vor mich.

That is too fancy for you;
it's in the big-city style;
we peasants don't sing so softly.
Listen to this number, which is the kind for me.

ARIA (BASS):
Es nehme zehntausend Ducaten der Kammerherr
  alle Tag' ein.
Er trink' ein gutes Gläschen Wein,
und lass' es ihm bekommen sein.

May the chamberlain take in ten thousand ducats
  every day.
May he drink a good glass of wine
and may it agree with him.

RECITATIVE (SOPRANO):
Das klingt zu liederlich.
Es sind so hübsche Leute da,
die würden ja
von Herzen drüber lachen;
nicht anders, als wenn ich
die alte Weise wollte machen:

That sounds too vulgar.
There are so many fine people present,
they would surely
laugh heartily at it;
exactly as if I
were to sing the old-fashioned tune:

ARIA (SOPRANO):
Gieb, Schöne,
viel Söhne
von art'ger Gestalt,
und zieh' sie fein alt,
das wünschet sich Zschocher und Knauthain
  fein bald.

Beautiful woman, bear
many sons
of handsome form
and raise them up well;
that's what Zschocher and Knauthain wish will
  happen soon.

RECITATIVE (BASS):
Du hast wohl recht.
Das Stückchen klingt zu schlecht;
ich muss mich also zwingen,
was Städtisches zu singen.

You're probably right.
My little song sounds too coarse;
and so I've got to force myself
to sing something in big-city style.

ARIA (BASS):
Dein Wachsthum sei feste und lache vor Lust.
Deines Herzens Trefflichkeit
hat dir selbst das Feld bereit,
auf dem du blühen musst.

May your growth be firm and laugh for joy.
Your heart's excellence
has itself prepared for you the field
on which you must blossom.

RECITATIVE (SOPRANO & BASS):
(SOP.:) Und damit sei es auch genung.
(BASS:) Nun müssen wir wohl einen Sprung
in unsrer Schenke wagen.
(SOP.:) Das heisst, du willst nur das noch sagen:

And let that be an end of it.
Now we can surely have a hop
in our tavern.
That means, you just want to add this:

ARIA (SOPRANO):
Und dass ihr's alle wisst,
es ist nunmehr die Frist
zu trinken.
Wer durstig ist, mag winken.
Versagt's die rechte Hand,
so dreht euch unverwandt
zur linken.

So that you may all know,
now is the time
to drink.
Whoever is thirsty, give a sign.
If the right hand refuses,
turn around resolutely
to the left.

RECITATIVE (BASS & SOPRANO):
(BASS:) Mein Schatz, errathen!
(SOP.:) Und weil wir nun dahier
nichts mehr zu thun, so wollen wir
auch Schritt vor Schritt
in unsre alte Schenke waten.
(BASS:) Ei! hol' mich der und dieser,
Herr Ludwig, und der Steu'r-Reviser
muss heute mit.

You guessed it, darling!
And since we now have
nothing more to do here, we will
make our way straight
to our old tavern.
Ho! I'll be damned, but
Mister Ludwig and the tax examiner
must come along today!

SOPRANO & BASS:
Wir gehn nun wo der Tudelsack
in unsrer Schenke brummt.
Und rufen dabei fröhlich aus:
Es lebe Dieskau und sein Haus,
ihm sei bescheert,
was er begehrt
und was er sich selbst wünschen mag.

We're now going where the bagpipe
drones in our tavern.
And, so doing, we call out merrily:
Long live Dieskau and his household;
may he be granted
all that he desires
and whatever he may wish for himself.

THE END